SELL
LEARN
REPEAT

The powerful secret to extraordinary and sustainable business growth.

CRAIG BALLARD

SELL   LEARN   REPEAT

A POWERFUL SYSTEM FOR EXTRAORDINARY AND SUSTAINABLE BUSINESS GROWTH

CRAIG BALLARD

Copyright © 2018 Craig Ballard
All rights reserved.

ISBN: 1719358230
ISBN 13: 978-1719358231

TABLE OF CONTENTS

Preface, Foreword, & About The Author 9

Part 1 – Warming Up 21

Chapter 1: It Ain't Rocket Science 23
Chapter 2: You Don't Have a Sales Problem 28
Chapter 3: Don't Take Knowledge to a Process Fight .. 35
Chapter 4: Without Measurement & Discipline, you are Pucked 49
Chapter 5: The Sales Manager is Dead...................... 54
Chapter 6: Being Great Isn't Good Enough.................. 68
Chapter 7: Ballard's Rule of Two 72

Part 2 - The SELL·LEARN·REPEAT Sales Growth System 81

Chapter 8: Sell·Learn·Repeat is easy as PIE 83
Chapter 9: MAP 91
Chapter 10: TARGET 97
Chapter 11: ENGAGE 102
Chapter 12: PROPOSE 108
Chapter 14: CLOSE 117

Chapter 15: ADAPT 128
Chapter 16: REPEAT, REPEAT, REPEAT…REPEAT, AGAIN 139

Part 3 – Really Advanced Concepts 143

Chapter 17: Revenue is Overrated 147
Chapter 18: Build Sales Growth & ROI Metrics 152
Chapter 19: Hunters & Huggers 163
Chapter 20: Ballard's 50/1 Rule 169
Chapter 21: Ballard's 3rd Law of Diminishing Chart Returns.. 174
Chapter 22: Ballard's 4th Law of Really Good Guys & Gals.. 178
Chapter 23: That Sugar Won't Fly Anymore 181
Chapter 24: For Serious Cases Only 186

Preface, Foreword, & About The Author

Don't worry - this isn't going to take long. I combined all the preamble into one section because according to my publisher, I don't get paid by the page. I was going to have Stephen Covey write my foreword but he backed out at the last minute when his assistant's assistant wouldn't return my calls. Plus he's 114 years old and has been cryogenically frozen for 12 years, so his forewords aren't as peppy as they used to be.

The 8th Habit of Highly Effective People

"Bill, you should really read the 7 Habits of Highly Effective People - it will change your life!"

If you wanted a 300 page book with appendices and footnotes, this ain't it. Textbooks are for teachers. This book is for DOERS. I'm not going to use 300 pages to explain something that you should be able to grasp with 50, and a few pictures to spice it up. I have a day job.

- Do you request the longest route when you get directions on Google Maps?
- Do you feel ripped off if your root canal only takes 10 minutes and doesn't hurt?
- Do you wish porn movies had more plot development?
- Do you spend 4 years in University to get a degree in Geography?[1]

Well all right then.

Books and ideas aren't like pistachios, or chicken wings, or Sophia Vergara[2] where more is better.

The point is to transfer the information as quickly and as painlessly as possible.

---

[1] Sorry, that was a cheap shot.
[2] You can substitute Channing Tatum if you must.

This is the ADD generation, so I'm going to try and keep it short and pithy so you don't start snap chatting your choochy[3] or whatever it is millennials do all day when they aren't being ironic.

This book is for busy, serious sales professionals, sales leaders, CEO's, business owners and organizations that want to get much better at growing revenue in a predictable, consistent, repeatable fashion. In fact, it's for all people in any line of work that need to grow something important to them.

Let's broaden the definition a bit:

SALES = OUTCOMES that matter to you or your organization.

Maybe that's donors to the Opera House. Maybe it's the number of volunteers for your charity or nerds in your Big Bang Theory viewing club.

Maybe it's how many snowblowers you are selling in Sault St. Marie or how many Billy's Buffalo Burger franchises you want to sell in Tennessee.

---

[3] I don't really know what a 'choochy' is. I'm pretty sure its dirty. Use your imagination.

It doesn't matter what the product or service is. It doesn't matter whether it's for profit or not. It doesn't matter if you are a landscaper with one mower or a global conglomerate with 10,000 employees in 55 countries. - whether you make 50K a year, 500K or 5 zillion.

I don't care what your title is or what you did before. If you aren't achieving double digit growth every single year with confidence, then you need help.

If you don't want to grow your revenues or your subscriptions or memberships, then you are on the wrong train. This one is moving.

Sales mediocrity and anemic revenue growth doesn't discriminate between big companies or small, new or old, Silicon Valley or Gasoline Alley. (that's in Red Deer, Alberta[4] for those playing at home).

The system, principals and process laid out in this book will work EVERY TIME if you are serious about sales growth. If you aren't, no book is going to help you, so get back to the couch or to your sales meeting, which is probably more comfortable.

My name is Craig Ballard. I am an entrepreneur and CEO of growth focused companies and I give advice to companies that

---

[4] Alberta is in Canada. That's a country. Above the US. Two above Mexico.

struggle to grow their revenues organically, which is a fancy of way of saying they aren't very good at selling their own products or services in a sustainable or extraordinary fashion.

I have built companies from scratch and sold them to much larger companies like GE. I have had great successes and some doozy failures - like as in worse than a 'code brown' when I used to clean the bathrooms at McDonalds. I have been involved in sales either as a buyer or seller for the last thirty years in one form or another, from selling newspaper subscriptions door to door when I was 12, to complex long term consulting projects, and everything you can imagine in between. Widgets, Wedgies, and One-Eyed Winkle berries (which are delicious).

Whatever the industry, whatever the product or service - I have found a way to profitably grow revenues faster than my competition. OK, yes, you can call me the Growth Whisperer. I know that's what you were thinking.

Supply chain management software, aircraft parts management, 3rd Party Logistics, handheld payment terminals, transaction processing, hospital billing systems, batteries and renewable energy - the list goes on.

I have learned things the hard way. I have done a lot of things that have worked, and plenty that haven't. I have fallen into the same pits as everybody else, but usually not the same pit more than twice.

I have also read a lot of books about sales and growing revenue (I never counted, but I will swag it between 100 and 200 books on this subject). An exceedingly small number of those have been helpful. One of my all-time favourites is the Ultimate Sales Machine by the late great Chet Holmes.

Other than my book, this is the only one I recommend, and no, I don't get a spiff from his estate. Many of them are painfully derivative or written by folks who spent more time at overpriced consulting firms than in the trenches with real customers or salespeople.

Most books or courses on sales focus on what I would call sales acumen or technique, the tactical side of how you go about selling a product or service within the context of a single sales cycle. This is domain knowledge and a lifelong profession.

I'm not going to teach you how to catch the big one. When to give him some slack, when to reel him in, how to be his friend and listen to him, or when to whack him on the head with a little baseball bat.

I'm going to teach you how to build a fishing machine that will work with every kind of fisherman and fish, from the gimpy to the gifted, and from the guppy's to the gator's.

So, although it gets the most attention with gurus, literature and seminars - **individual sales ability is the least important part of improving your sales growth**.

There are thousands of books on how to get better at winning the customer and getting the big deal.

But they won't help you grow your business in a predictable, consistent, repeatable fashion. If they did, you wouldn't need me.

The most important concept we need to establish for you to get the results you want is that **sales growth is a process.** Even, if that is all you take away from this book, then I still can sleep at night.

In fact, I can save you the thousands of hours and dollars I have poured into traditional sales books looking for great wisdom and summarize 99% of them right here with a few sentences:

1. Find out what customers want, and then (wait for it...) give it to them.

2. Become a trusted advisor to your customer by focusing on their needs. This is also called "consultative selling", but if you need 300 pages of babble or a 4 hour seminar to figure that out, maybe your destiny is more foam packing peanuts than sales.

3. Don't deal with people you hate or that wouldn't piss on you if you were on fire.

You're welcome. Now Let's get after it.

I don't want this book to end up propping up your wobbly patio furniture. I want it to be the beacon that serves as your guiding light in sales for generations. A man can dream.

For the same cost as a fancy coffee and treat at your local foofy hipster cafe, you can pour something even more delicious and valuable into your blood stream - the concepts in this book that will grow revenue like you never thought possible.

Plus if you are a fast reader, you can finish it while drinking a Venti. If you aren't into coffee than you probably aren't into sales, but don't worry, if you want to drink a luke warm cold pressed glass of organic[5] yak turds instead, knock yourself out.

---

[5] No Mr. Know It All, not all poop is organic. You have to specify. Some genetically modified Yaks can now make synthetic poop and only a trained palette can tell the difference.

Part 1 – Warming Up

Chapter 1:
It Ain't Rocket Science

If it was, do you think you could buy it for 9.99 and read the whole thing while drinking your latte you cheap bastard[6]?

Not too much these days is rocket science, other than, well, um - rocket science.

But the thing about 'gamechanging' ideas is that the ideas themselves are rarely all that revolutionary or mindblowing.

I'm pretty sure 99% of all books on diet over the last 20 years could be summed up by:

If you stop eating most simple carbohydrates, you will lose weight and probably be healthier and feel better.

---

[6] I'm not sure if 'bastard' is a unisex term. You don't really call women 'bastards'. We need another 'B' word for females. Umm, nothing is coming to me right now.

Anybody who doesn't know this by now has either been living in a cave without wifi or is waddling in line at Cinnebon right now. Don't get icing on your Kindle - it voids the warranty.

So, *knowing* what to do is the easy part.

We need gimmicks, we need breakthroughs - we need someone to inspire us and show us the light - the eureka moment where you nod your head and think, holy crap - I literally have been living a lie - I thought Brangelina was forever!

We need it to be put in compelling bite sized chunks that we can consume while we are taking a picture of our organic locally grown and humanely chopped salad.

Nothing that you are about to read here is the caramilk secret. My life isn't in imminent danger by sharing this information. I don't think the squirrels are listening to my thoughts. At least not since I upped my dosage.

The society of sales guru's probably isn't plotting my accidental death. "Holy shit Ballard you crazy sob - you gave the whole freaking caboodle away!" They will write books after this one, and most of those will still suck balls.

However, disclaimers aside, if you take a moment to actually think about the things I'm going to tell you and then put them into action, in even a reasonably close semblance to how I have described, then I know you will get results.

And if you cut out most simple carbs in your diet, you will get results.

And if you need 10 more diet books to tell you the same thing, or you keep having mediocre sales growth after reading this, then I feel bad taking your 9.99. Not bad enough to give you a refund, but still sort of bad.

Ok, I'm over it. It's time to stop searching for magic powder and get your head out of your ass. If I inspire one out of 100 readers to actually DO the things I'm going to talk about, then it will have been worth it.

Are you going to be that 1?

Let's find out B Word.

TATER THOUGHTS

"Being a consultant is like flying first-class. The food is terrific, the drinks are cold. But all you can do is walk up to the pilot and say, 'bank left.' If you're in management, you have the controls."

Greg Brenneman

Chapter 2: You Don't Have a Sales Problem.

Bold statement, right? And not a very smart one if you write books about sales, but don't worry about me - we're going to solve the real problem that is paralyzing your growth and evaporating your market share.

OK, I know you're intrigued now. The anticipation is palpable.

No, you don't have a sales problem - you have a *commitment* problem.

And no, this isn't going to be a male bashing session.

By commitment problem, I mean you or your organization are not committed to doing the boring, repetitive, necessary process driven things that lead to sales growth and instead spend a lot of time trying to find secret potions that will solve everything or making excuses about why you can't grow.

Here's the number 1 reason why most companies are not growing organically today:

Drumroll please...

1. They don't engage with their customers enough.

How much engagement is enough? For most organizations, probably 5-10X the amount you are doing today, unless of course you are doing zero (because 5 X 0 = 0, get it?), which believe it or not is true for a lot of companies of all sizes.

If you aren't holding your salespeople accountable for engaging with customers as the most important measure of their performance, then you just don't care, or you're lazy, or you lack cajones, or all of the above.

You are not committed to sales growth.

And now, as they say in the old folks home, get ready for Number 2!

The second reason most companies are not growing organically today is:

2. They have no consistent repeatable feedback loop.

If you don't track when you meet or interact with customers in a DATABASE of some kind, and document the outcomes of those interactions, then you don't care, or you aren't serious about sales, or you are going to be looking for a new opportunity soon.

You are not committed to sales growth.

A database doesn't have to be a fancy or expensive CRM - that's just another excuse or smokescreen or what I like to call 'bullshit'.

I can get on your computer and set up a decent CRM for you in 5 minutes, and that's if I get distracted and start snap chatting my cat doing the dab at the same time.

So, if you are committed to meeting with real live customers where they work (not at trade shows - that doesn't count) at dramatically higher levels than you do today, and are committed to keeping track of those interactions and their outcomes in a database (a less scary word than CRM), then you no longer have a commitment problem.

The rest is execution, and that's what the rest of the book is going to help you with.

Once you are committed, all things are possible.

TATER THOUGHTS

"When it comes to sales growth, the buck starts and stops at the very top of the organization. If the owners or CEO aren't constantly reinforcing the culture and expectations throughput the organization and instead are relying entirely on their sales leaders to get the job done, then they shouldn't be surprised when the results fall short. If you are the leader – you are accountable for sales – period."

Craig Ballard

Chapter 3: Don't Take Knowledge to a Process Fight

This is going to piss off some old timers out there, but what's the point of life if you can't make some old grumpy dudes mad every once in awhile? I'm going to be one soon so I have to get my digs in while I can.

Domain knowledge is the understanding and mastery of a specific subject matter. Say like, you know the automotive aftermarket parts industry or you know how to catch a wide mouth bass or you are a great hockey player.

You may also know how to develop rapport with a client or ask the right questions during a sales meeting. You may also know all the most important trade shows to attend.

Domain knowledge is often developed over many years with education, training, and of course experience.

Up until probably 15 years ago or thereabouts, domain knowledge was still the most valuable currency in business and probably government as well.

But, them darn computers and the interwebs messed everything up, and now domain knowledge, while still valuable, is much easier and cheaper to acquire.

I was at one of my favourite Japanese restaurants in Toronto recently enjoying the Tepenyaki treatment. That's where you all sit around a blazing hot stainless steel grill and an authentic Japanese chef prepares your food on the grill right there in front of you.

They do all sorts of cool stuff and make volcano's out of onion rings and flip eggs with their spatula and then they juggle their spatulas - and they crack some well rehearsed jokes. I highly recommend it. Their skill and dedication is impressive.

I asked one of the chefs - who clearly had what seemed like a thick Japanese accent and who had obviously been studying his art since he was in diapers (which in Japanese is called sakapupu) - I asked him where did he learn this amazing talent.

I was expecting him to say that it had been passed on over 100's of years or that he went to a special institute in Okinawa where he had to walk on hot steel grills barefoot for 10 years before they would even let him near a spatula, and then when he got the spatula, he had to sleep with it, shower with it, fight to the death with it, etc. for another 10 years before he became a busboy. You get the idea.

Well, turns out his training wasn't quite that involved.

In fact, his answer was as follows:

Rutube!

And he yelled it out loud with honour and dignity and a hint of anger, which is also the perfect combination of Japanese emotions.

Sorry, did you say 'roo-tube'?

No, ROOTUBE!

Now he looked like he might come across the grill at me with a flying death spatula to the throat, but then the lightbulb went off.

Oh, you mean YOUTUBE?

Yes, ROOTUBE!

You learned all this crazy shit on YOUTUBE?

ROOTUBE

Although the food was still delicious, a little piece of my surrogate Japanese soul died that day, because my authentic

Japanese chef learned his art on YouTube, from watching other Japanese masters who also apparently have a GoPro.

The point is, domain knowledge is still important, but it can be acquired SO much faster, and more cheaply than it could even 10 years ago.

So, here's something you need to accept if you don't want to suck: I can learn 80% of everything you know in your domain in less than 10% of the time it took you to acquire it and my knowledge will be more up to date and less susceptible to confirmation bias.

And don't get all butt hurt - you can say the exact same thing to me.

We are all in the same boat, or butt if you will.

The half-life of our experience advantage is getting much, much shorter.

You don't have 30 years of experience in the automotive aftermarket parts industry - you have 2 years, 15 times over. That isn't to say there isn't any knowledge worth acquiring that can take more than 20 minutes or 2 years, just that knowledge is a much more efficient and free market today thanks to technology. The barriers to acquiring knowledge are far lower.

I can tell you the sales folks at Encyclopedia Brittanica weren't too thrilled with Wikipedia.

If you want to master any important discipline in business, including sales growth, you and your company need **process knowledge.**

Processes are a series of steps that you follow to complete a task or to achieve a goal.

It's no more complicated than that.

Processes are often independent of the domain to which they are applying. They are transferrable, repeatable, and scalable, they often offer economies of scale - which is to say that the more you do the process, the more powerful it becomes. We'll talk more about that later.

And processes offer one other really important thing for your business. If followed with discipline, *they lead to predictable results.*

Today, mastering and implementing processes that work is harder than acquiring domain knowledge, but it lasts much longer and is much harder to copy because it requires sustained discipline.

Discipline is a quality in very short supply in most companies and leadership. It's also why everybody doesn't look like a fitness model. Knowing what to do and actually doing it are two different things.

OK - let's keep moving. Processes are ultimately much more powerful than domain knowledge.

And here's why.

I have met many successful and wealthy business owners, some of whom I consider close friends, and in most cases, they have achieved their success through many years of acquiring and exploiting domain knowledge, and usually in a single domain.

Let's use plumbing parts distribution as an example.

Bill knows everything there is to know about valves and gaskets, pipes and fitting, faucets and tubs. He grew up in the business, and built it up with his family over 30 years.

Bob has built a really successful plumbing distribution business. He knows everybody in the industry and he knows the plumbing game inside and out. He's a big player in his town.

Do you think Bill could jump over to a wood products or sporting goods company and get similar results?

Probably not. Because Bill's most valuable knowledge isn't really about the *process* of wholesale distribution, its specific to the plumbing business.

In today's global and real-time economy, where we can access information and data so quickly, from anywhere in the world, learning about the ins and outs of plumbing parts and all the key players in the industry and their strengths and weaknesses doesn't take that long.

Generally speaking, most domain knowledge (80% of almost any domain) can be picked up in a year or two by a reasonably astute smart cookie (RASC, for you acronym lovers or AL's). OK, RASCALS fine - that just happened.

Knowing the key processes that drive successful wholesale distribution, regardless of the industry, is the knowledge that is far more scalable and that can be transferred to ANY industry.

The sales growth process we are going to talk about can be applied to any industry, and now is the time to get it through your head (assuming you have pulled it out of your ass already) that if you are going to build anything great, that can grow to any size, you will need more process knowledge than domain knowledge, and **those that understand the difference will be far more successful than their peers.**

Just to hammer the point home a little further, here's a table that shows some examples of the differences between domain and process knowledge.

Figure 1: Domain vs Process Knowledge

Domain	Process
Burgers	McDonalds
Graphic Arts	Marketing
Lug Nuts	Purchasing
Creativity	Innovation
Actor	Producer
Knowing	Learning
Ends	Means
Selling	Sales Growth

Now, of course general sales acumen is transferrable to a variety of industries, as are other business disciplines, but that doesn't mean they are processes.

Remember, processes are also repeatable, scalable, offer economies of scale, and lead to predictable results.

Chad is a great sales guy, and he can sell Hyundai's or Hotcakes, but Chad isn't a process. Chad is one guy. And if Chad gets hit by a bus, Chad's company is probably screwed for awhile, especially if it was their bus.

I repeat, Chad is not a process (sorry Chad - you're still a great guy!)

If you take one thing away from this chapter:

Don't take knowledge to a process fight. Sales growth is a process fight.

TATER THOUGHTS

"If you can't describe what you are doing as a process, you don't know what you are doing"

W. Edwards Deming

Chapter 4: Without Measurement & Discipline, you are Pucked[7]

Ok, so if you are still reading, it's because you are truly committed to organic sales growth and you believe deeply in your soul that sales growth is a process. A process you need to master.

That still isn't enough, because if you aren't measuring what you are doing in a disciplined fashion, it ain't going to be worth a weasel shart in a shitstorm - as my old grandpappy used to say.

---

[7] This is a Canadian term. It means being hit by a puck. For example, "Hey Bruce, I heard you got pucked in the face last night", or if you flung a puck at Bruce's mom, you'd be a motherpucker. Visitors to Canada be careful with this, because it sounds like 'plucked' and that's a very offensive term to Canadians. There's no direct translation in English but it basically means you shave your rear end with a dirty razor. Needless to say, you should never call someone a motherplucker unless you are prepared to drop the gloves.

The Quick and Dirty Ballard Sales Test

If you have salespeople and you can't show me a report within 3 minutes of exactly what they all did last month and exactly how it benefited your organization, then you can't measure what you are doing. And if you can't measure the inputs and outcomes of your process, then how are you going to know if it's working, or how to make it better?

Why are you even doing it if you aren't going to measure it and report it publicly?

I'm not talking about call logs or emails, or "Had lunch with Garth". I'm talking about real, useful, actionable information about how the market is responding to your value proposition.

Not just last month, but every month. Not sometimes, but all the time and for all time.

If you don't have the information at your fingertips right now and you are a sales leader or CEO then clean out your desk and get out, but leave this book so the next person has half a chance.

Measurement takes discipline and follow-up and it cannot be optional.

There is nothing more important to your sales growth than the discipline of constant measurement and reporting.

You don't need a fancy CRM. You need to grow a pair (sorry ladies, I think that's a unisex term now with the whole Kaitlyn Jenner thing) and make it mandatory for everyone in your sales organization, whether it's in a spreadsheet or Salesforce, or Netsuite, or wherever.[8]

And if they aren't on board, then send them over to your competition so they can suck his resources while you find some people that won't suck yours. Fine, that came out wrong.

This concept is so simple, we don't need to spend any more time on it. If you can't understand why you need to measure the key inputs and outputs of your most important processes, then you should be reading a book with more pictures and less words.

---

[8] In the time it took me to write this sentence another 12 CRM apps have been launched.

TATER THOUGHTS

"Whatever it is in business, if you don't have the discipline to consistently and accurately measure the inputs and outputs, whether in a fancy cloud based app or on the back of a napkin, then your organization will know you aren't really serious about it."

Craig Ballard

Chapter 5:
The Sales Manager is Dead

If you currently fashion yourself a sales manager, my condolences, because you died about 15 years ago and your colour is not good at all. In fact, your skin is falling onto my expensive rugs. I'm going to have to ask you not to shed in my office.

Don't despair. You had a very, very good run. You went to a lot of trade shows and sent lots of emails and ate an epic amount of lunch, played a lot of golf. You got to go on a lot of nice trips or wink wink 'boondoggles'.

The days of the most capable salesperson working their way up to 'management' are officially over.

There is some really good news. There are still opportunities for important supporting roles in sales, *but they are different.*

So, we need to replace the old M word (**M**anager) with five new M words. These are the REAL SALES M Words. The ones that **M**atter.

There are five things of value (not so coincidentally all starting with M) you can do to support the sales process other than selling something (that's still the most valuable thing in case you were wondering), and yes, the size of the circles below is indicative of their relative and absolute value.

Figure 2: The Real Sales M Words

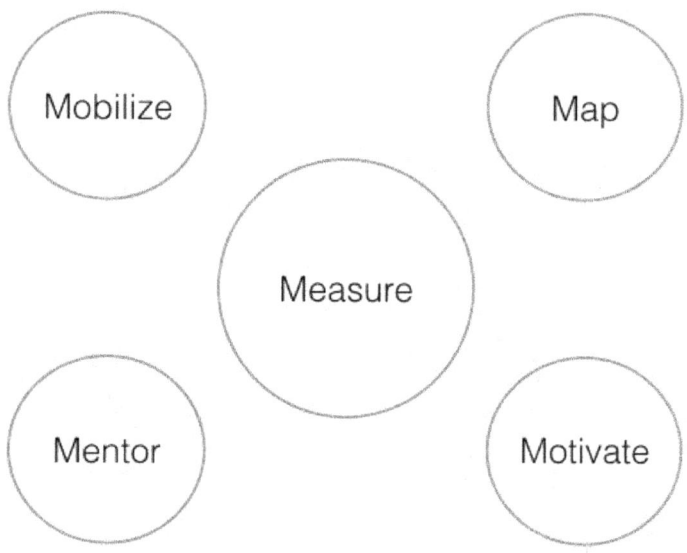

You can be a **Sales MAPPER.** This is the person or people that have a data map of every market that you sell to – they maintain an accurate, complete and up to date database of every potential customer - their location, size, decision making hierarchy, preferences, current suppliers, and priority to your organization. They know exactly what your market share is, and how the market breaks down by competing suppliers and brands. We'll talk more about MAPPING in Chapter 9.

You can be a **Sales MOBILIZER**. This is the person that attracts, finds, evaluates, and hires the right types of sales professionals you need to grow your business. They put the right sales butts in the right sales seats, wherever they are needed most in your organization. They know how to separate the closers from the posers – and make sure that anyone that gets into your organization and is representing your company is going to have the traits to be successful with a **process driven sales culture.**

You can be a **Sales MENTOR**. This is leading by example and showing the less experienced or talented sales people how its done in the streets. Ride along with me and I will show you how I sell - I will give you tips on what to do in these types of situations and show you some of the techniques and methods that have helped me sell.

But this person's main job is still SELLING. She might be a team captain but she's still on the ice, scoring goals and digging pucks in the corners. They are really good at what they do, and they tend to work best alone.

You can be a **Sales MOTIVATOR**. You are great at whipping up a group of people into a frenzy and inspiring them to give it

110% - to believe in the cause - go the extra mile, win that trip to Reno.

But this person's main job is also still SELLING. He might make a higher base salary and be a rainmaker in getting the big deals done, but motivating isn't a full time job or at least it shouldn't be if you hire the right sales people.

Last, not least, you can be a **Sales MEASURER** which is arguably the most important role in any company that wants to grow and is essential to succeeding with the SELL·LEARN·REPEAT approach.

The skills and aptitude required to be successful in this role are totally different than the skill sets of most traditional Sales Managers, and unlike the other supporting functions, this is a full time job.

This is a person that lives and breathes process, data, measurement, and discipline. These are qualities of more left brain dominant folks. This is the referee - the scorekeeper - *the oracle of knowledge that is built from processes.* This is the band manager, not the lead guitarist.

Think Velma, not Fred, Daphne, Shaggy or Scoobie.

And here's a SELL·LEARN·REPEAT wake up call. Most really good sales people don't have these qualities. In fact, these are often their biggest weaknesses. They are more right brain folks. They have other gifts.

So, why would you ask a right brain to do a left brain job?

You wouldn't, but most companies have been doing exactly that since the beginning of sales.[9]

The best athletes in a sport rarely make the best coaches or managers. Apples and oranges. Why do we think business would be any different?

If someone tells you they aspire to be a Sales Manager - then ask them to show you all the ways they have built repeatable processes, discipline, and measurement into their sales job.

Ask them to explain how they can add value to the real Sales M words, including evidence of their track record with specific examples from their career.

If they can't, then you know they have little to offer in a sales support role.

I know what you are thinking. 'Ok smart guy - who do the sales people report to? Who hires them and fires them and holds them accountable?

Who gets to be the big boss man who has the biggest salary and nicest car and the extra large suite at the Sheraton?

---

[9] Our best guess on the first sale ever was when a cavemen sold his magic flame to a rival caveman down the river. Well, he didn't really sell it, he traded it for this circular rolling rock the other dude came up with. Eventually they became partners, and called their company 'Firestone'. The rest is history.

This is the outdated mentality of a lot of people who get into sales. I will be a really good salesperson, I will put in my time pounding the pavement, and eventually, I will get to be a Manager, and after that a Director, and maybe even a VP one day, which is the only path for me to make the big bucks, and stop these dogs from barking.

In other words, I will be so good at sales that I will be way too important to actually have to sell stuff.

The person who makes the most money in the SELL-LEARN-REPEAT organization will be the one who *sells the most*.

She may well be accountable to someone who makes considerably less, and doesn't even have a company car.

Finding ultra-talented and motivated sales people is much harder than finding people that can measure sales activity and processes and hold people accountable.

You need to get over this.

If you are a salesperson, this should be a powerful and emancipating concept.

You don't have to be the sales manager to make the most money or have the prestige or title or corner office.

You have to be really good at selling.

Someone less expensive than you will do all the important M Word things that makes sales growth a process, and they will be happy to do that job.

OK, right, but who do the salespeople report to?

It's not that important if they are accountable to a process and an individual that oversees that process, as long as that process is supported from the very top of the organization.

So, they can be accountable to the Sales Measurement Leader (SML), and report to the head of their business unit, but **do not** have them report to someone who is better with doughnuts than data.

And don't have them report to anybody whose main focus is selling, because it will add no value to either party, and worse, be a distraction to your rainmakers.

Are there good salespeople who can also be good at sales measurement? Yes - it happens - even a blind squirrel finds a nut - and then you have a very special resource who has a rare combination of left and right brain strengths, and they will be very expensive.

It would be tempting to try and find these types of people to be your 'Sales Manager', but don't give in to the temptation. It will just give you another excuse why you aren't succeeding.

You don't need that unicorn, unless it jumps in your lap, and if you know what a unicorn is, you probably don't want it jumping directly into your lap.

With a strong SML, who can be both cheerleader and ass-kicker when the situation calls for it, you will be just fine. Think of this person more like the head trainer than head coach. They are there to track your performance and help you succeed, but they aren't marshmallows that will put up with crap.

If you don't have a dedicated Sales Mobilizer role in your company, the SML can also huddle with the existing sales team, and especially the most experienced folks, to help recruit and evaluate new members for the team.

You don't need a fancy sales manager for that, and once again, being good at sales is not the same things as being good at identifying and attracting good sales people. Recruiting (Mobilizing) is a process, and remember, right brained rainmakers are not good with processes.

The SML will cost much less than a traditional sales manager, and offer far more ROI to your organization.

Are you over it? Are you with me?

Are you a recovering Sales Manager that has no aptitude for processes, measurement, and discipline?

Don't worry, you can go back to sales and make lots of money, as long as you aren't too proud now to sell.

This is what great sales people do. They sell.

TAKEAWAY: Stop wasting your time and money trying to find that elusive unicorn that can be great at both sales mentorship and sales measurement. Keep you best sales people in front of customers, growing revenue. Find someone great at managing and measuring processes to hold sales people accountable, and don't worry, they probably won't make nearly as much as your best sales people.

TATER THOUGHTS

"Real sales people live to compete and win – they want to be in the game. Doesn't matter their age or experience. Don't make your best sales people into sales managers – that's like making Connor McDavid or Lebron James head coach of their team. Why would you want players like that on the sidelines? A real Sales Manager is a process and measurement oriented role and requires very different skills and aptitudes than a great sales person. It's very important, just like the head coach, but the people putting pucks in the net should be getting the biggest checks."

Craig Ballard

Chapter 6: Being Great Isn't Good Enough.

This one is going to be shorter and sweeter than Selena Gomez[10].

There's a lot of people in sales who are 'great' guys or girls. Some of these people even have some leadership qualities.

People like them. They want to be around them. They can be charming and magnetic.

Beware the great guys and girls.

Many of them (not all) cannot manage their time and follow a process to save their life, let alone keep track of their activities in a database, so they rely purely on relationships and their

---

[10] Justin Beiber if you must. Tom Cruise for the old school ladies. Emmanuel Lewis if you're weird.

silver tongues, but that won't do anymore. It will not sustain your business for the long haul or build competitive advantage.

That said, you may be able to teach these dogs new tricks, and to follow your process with discipline.

Many won't be able to keep up or will resist and push back.

So, no matter how great these guys and girls are, if they can't drink your kool-aid and get with the program, they cannot stay.

For any process or system to work, you need 100% commitment and buy-in from everyone the process touches, and especially the sales team.

If even one person isn't holding their end up, it threatens the entire system and undermines its authority and legitimacy.

The natives will get restless. They can smell double standards and hypocrisy like my wife can smell a fake Louis Vuitton purse (which I had to take back to the alley where I bought it).

Still not convinced? Check out Ballard's 4th Law in Chapter 22 and I think you'll be drinking my brand of Kool-Aid before it's all said and done.

TATER THOUGHTS

"Grey doesn't scale. No matter how great you think someone is in sales, if they can't get with the program and follow a disciplined and repeatable process for growth, they have to go – no exceptions."

Craig Ballard

Chapter 7: Ballard's Rule of Two

Never, ever, EVER have only one salesperson in an important market

I saved this one for the end of Part 1 because a lot of people skip to the end, and this one is really important and one that many companies get wrong to their peril. Sometimes to their ultimate failure.

I'm going to make a bold statement and you are going to stick it in your pipe and smoke it. If you don't have a pipe, find somewhere good to stick it, and ummm…smoke it.

OK, here goes, repeat after me:

If you can't afford two salespeople for an important territory or for your entire business, then you can't afford any.

This the Ballard Rule of 2. It is absolute. There are no exceptions and I'm about to explain why. You can stop smoking it now. I hope you inhaled.

If you only have one salesperson in a market selling your products or services, regardless of the process, how will you know if they are doing well?

Let's say you have Vinni in New York (what, there's no sales guys in New York named Vinni?) and you are in the sauce business.

OK, Vinni has been working with you for 2 years in this key territory and he has sold $500K worth of sauce.

How is Vinni doing?

Well, what do you mean? Vinni is a great guy!

Nope, don't even start with me with that crap. We already went over that.

How is Vinni actually DOING?

Well, he must be doing pretty good - he sold 500K worth of sauce in a year.

Hmmm…but doing pretty good *compared to who*?

What if I told you that the average sauce salesperson in New York sold $1M worth of sauce in a year. What would you say now?

Is Vinnie still doing pretty good?

You have no benchmark or frame of reference from which to objectively judge Vinnie.

You have all your eggs in Vinnie's basket. Made you visualize it.

Vinne isn't just your best damn sauce salesperson in New York, he's also your ONLY one.

If you at least had Sal in uptown and Vinnie in midtown, and both those areas had a critical mass of sauce customers (not exactly the same amount, but enough to support their sales activity for a year), then you would have a much better idea of how Vinnie was doing.

Sal sold $300K in a year, and Vinnie sold $500K.

We don't know if Vinnie is the best sauce seller in the world, but we know he is selling more than Sal.

That is ONE data point more than we had before, and it is **incredibly valuable**, because without it, we cannot know whether it is the horse or the jockey that is winning or costing us the race.

If Vinnie and Sal are both struggling with the sauce sales, then is it possible that our sauce just ain't that good? Yes, it is, and there is some legitimacy to this hypothesis.

If it's just Vinnie, and he says nobody likes the sauce, then how do you know what to believe?

OK, but what if Vinnie is exceeding your wildest expectations. You can't make sauce fast enough to keep up with Vinnie's sales. Do you still need Sal?

You need Sal more than ever, because when one person controls an entire market for your business, you are incredibly vulnerable.

Vinnie could leave to your sauce arch rival. Vinnie could get hit by a bus. Vinnie could win the lottery and start that spiducci truck business he has been dreaming about.

And then you really are pucked,

But Craig, I can only afford to spend 60K on sales this year. I can't afford two people.

I'm a small business. We have a budget. Blah, blah, blah.

If you can afford to spend 60K a year on something for which you have no basis for measuring its effectiveness, or which could put you in an untenable position should that resource go away, then you can afford to spend 120K on something that you can measure, and for which you won't be left with your pants around your ankles if somebody jumps ship.

So, if you can't afford 120K, then you can't afford your own sales people yet, or you can't do sales in that territory yet.

Either do it yourself if you are an owner, or don't participate in that territory until you are in a position where you can do it right.

Whether you are a small family sauce company in Brooklyn or a much larger technology company deciding on whether you should expand to the West Coast, be wary of Vinnie's basket.

You know what I meant.

TATER THOUGHTS

"If you can't afford at least two sales people, you can't afford any. Maybe it's him or her or maybe it's your product or market, but you will never know for sure if you only have one data point."

Craig Ballard

Part 2 - The SELL·LEARN·REPEAT Sales Growth System

Chapter 8: Sell·Learn·Repeat is easy as PIE[11]

Let's make things even easier. We're going to break SELL·LEARN·REPEAT into seven simple steps – like a pie with six parts, and the seventh part? REPEAT!

Every single sales opportunity follows the same seven steps. And the more you repeat the process, the smarter and more powerful your sales and growth machine becomes.

Remember at the very beginning of the book which wasn't that long ago, I said: **Sales Growth is a Process.** And we can expand on that a bit now, and it will still fit in the overhead bin:

Sales growth is a *repeatable* process *with measurable results*.

---

[11] Who doesn't like pie?

If you follow it with conviction and discipline, you will get results – every time. It is certifiably effective. It is also Ballard Certified – which is like 10 times harder than ISO 9001[12].

And true Closers (more to come on that), which is not the same as your current definition of 'closer', *GET* SELL·LEARN·REPEAT which is to say they understand it. They buy into it. It is in their DNA. They are soldiers in the Sell·Learn·Repeat revolution.

They drink SELL·LEARN·REPEAT 24 x 7 x 365. (Which isn't easy)

My goal of this book is to make you and every sales person in your organization a real closer, not the Hollywood stereotype, and for you to adopt the tenets of the SELL·LEARN·REPEAT sales growth system.

I don't care if you call it Unga Bunga or Vulvamax, as long as you are doing it with discipline and consistency.

If you call it SELL·LEARN·REPEAT or use the term SELL·LEARN·REPEAT or even dream about SELL·LEARN·REPEAT - you will be hearing from my lawyer.

That's a joke. It's all yours for your own personal use - you paid the 9.99.

Behold - The SEVEN Essential & Delicious Steps of SELL·LEARN·REPEAT

---

[12] Perhaps like ISO 90010 or Seven Sigma. Yeah, I know – you thought there was only 6 – wussy.

This has its own page with a special tab so you can easily refer to it at any time. Do not stare directly at the SELL·LEARN·REPEAT process directly for more than a few seconds, as its sheer awesomeness could make you go blind or blow your brain out your ears. Remember, when it comes to charts and visuals, less is more. More on that for keeners like you in Chapter 21.

SELL·LEARN·REPEAT

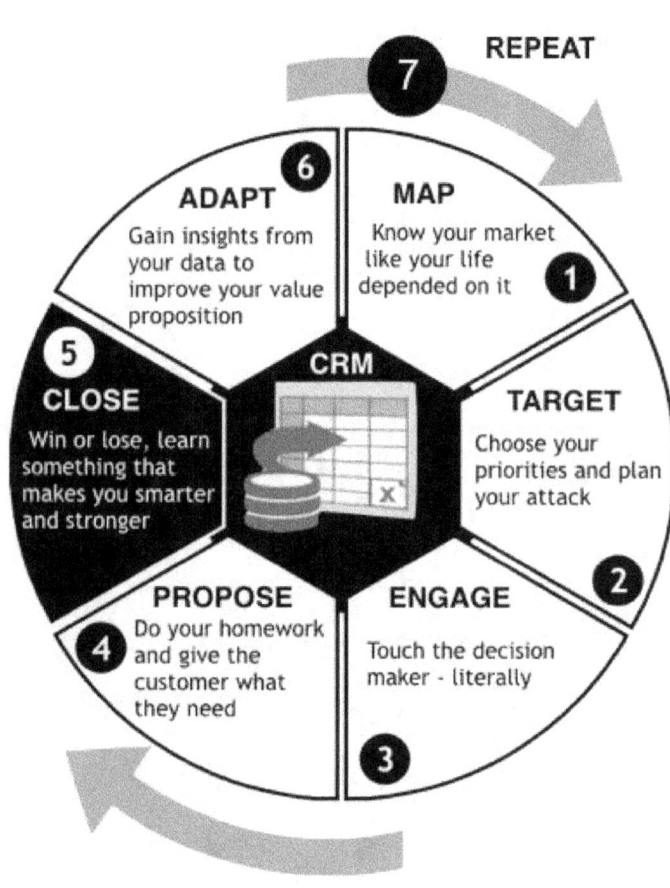

1. MAP

Find out exactly who your potential customers are in your chosen markets, and then catalogue all their important information in a database.

2. TARGET

Once you have mapped the markets you want to participate in, design a targeted campaign to prioritize and go after the ones that are most valuable to you.

3. ENGAGE

You know your market - you have planned a targeted attack. Now its time to engage the decision makers in that market with the most efficient and effective introduction you can make to your company. For many B2B companies, that will be meeting with a decision maker face to face. For other types of businesses, there are different approaches.

4. PROPOSE

Work with the qualified prospects to develop an informed proposal to meet their needs - one that is framed to your advantage wherever possible.

5. CLOSE

With SELL·LEARN·REPEAT, you will close every single qualified prospect. That doesn't mean you will win them all, but you won't lose a single one, because if you learn something valuable that can help your business from that interaction, you aren't losing. You will close the loop on every sales cycle and get the most valuable information to your business by getting a definitive answer on your proposal including why you won the business, or why you didn't.

6. ADAPT

Use all that precious feedback to adapt and refine your value proposition so that you will be stronger when you go back to those prospects and you strengthen your position relative to your competition.

7. REPEAT

This is almost like a bonus step I included for those that weren't sure where to go from here.

Here's a hint, its a circle, so there's only one place to go, and that's back to the beginning.

Start all over again, ***but get smarter every revolution***.

Seven basic fundamental steps to sales growth. I told you it wasn't rocket science. If you follow them religiously, you will grow your revenues faster than 99% of companies in the world and you will dominate your competition because they won't get it. They will hire some fancy overpriced consulting company or try to find unicorns and rainmakers or dudes who like hanging out at trade shows, but they will not change anything.

But you will, right?

As simple and incredibly straightforward as these steps obviously are, I'm going to describe each of them in a little more detail and provide an example here or there just because I'm that kind of standup guy. I'm also going to tell you some easy ways you can integrate these steps into any kind of CRM, whether in Excel or on the most expensive ERP on the planet.

TATER THOUGHTS

"If you wish to make an apple pie from scratch, you must first invent the universe."

Carl Sagan

Chapter 9: MAP

You can't get anywhere these days without a map. I'm not sure I could find my own house from 4 blocks away without my iPhone. We have outsourced our memories to our devices and the cloud, and no information, no matter how obscure is more than a Google search away. Of course if the internet goes down for more than a couple hours we'll all be sitting in our own poop in short order.

We can't even have the pleasure of having something on the tip of our tongue anymore.

Oh no he de-hint!

The first step in achieving consistent sales growth is knowing your market like the back of your hand, or in today's language, like the back of your IPhone. Or your Galaxy or Huawei, Android, or Atari, or whatever it is you use. Don't get all fake platform outraged on me.

Vinnie, and his boss, Frank, and the big boss Pauly, should all be able to tell me the following information within 5 minutes of me asking, which is long enough to open your laptop (well maybe 10 minutes for Windows), get into your software or the cloud, and show me the data.

- From the best information you have readily available (which is a lot) how many businesses in your service area (Manhattan) need pasta sauce.
- Where are they located (like on a real map)
- Who are the decision makers for those businesses and where do we reach them.
- What are the distribution channels to reach those businesses.
- How much sauce do they use per year (in gallons and $)
- How much of the market do you know about, e.g. have enough information to determine if they are a viable prospect.
- How much of the market is 'dark' to you - or where you don't have enough information to qualify them as a prospect.
- What is your estimate of the total market size that is relevant for your business.

- How many customers do you have and how many buy some of their sauce from you versus all.
- What is your total market share.

This is what I mean by a MAP. Sure, sometimes it is helpful to see the information geomapped, but that's not always relevant to your business.

All this information should be in a database or spreadsheet. You could use different coloured pushpins on a map if that works for you.

More sophisticated companies can integrate this database into their CRM's or ERP's.

OK, so here's a summary of what Pauly's map looks like:

Total Unique Buyers	2,000
Buyers I Know	1,000
Buyers I Don't Know	1,000
$ Value of the Know's	50,000,000
Estimated Total Market Value	100,000,000
Some Pauly's	80
All Pauly's	10
Total Pauly's Customers	90
Pauly's Sauce Sales Last 12 Months	1,800,000
Pauly's Market Share	1.8%

Of course, this summary all comes from a simple database of all buyers in the market.

This is a simple market map, and from here we can add more data points (competitors, sauce varieties, regions, demographics, etc.), to slice and dice the market in as many ways as is useful for our needs, but the more important point is that if you don't have something THIS SIMPLE as a starting point, then nothing else matters, because we will be like a blind doctor doing a prostate exam in the dark with a boxing glove. And trust me when I say you don't want to be getting that exam.

Everything starts with your MAP, and eventually returns to your MAP at the end of the process. As the MAP gets more complete and accurate, the better your sales efforts will become. Having an excellent MAP is very rare, and will be a competitive advantage for you and your company if you are committed to sales growth.

If you can't produce a MAP for me in 5 minutes (10 for Windows users), then we can't be friends, and worse yet, its a pre-requisite for the next step, TARGET.

Because what are we going to target without a MAP? As we say in Canada, that's like trying to shoot moose turds in a tornado[13].

---

[13] If you ever have to shoot moose turds in a tornado, try to aim for the frozen ones. Enough said.

Someone well organized, detail oriented and good with data needs to be in charge of the MAP. Which means it probably isn't going to be someone good at sales.

Oh yes he did.

TATER THOUGHTS

"If you don't know where you are going, don't be surprised when you get there."

Craig Ballard

Chapter 10:
TARGET

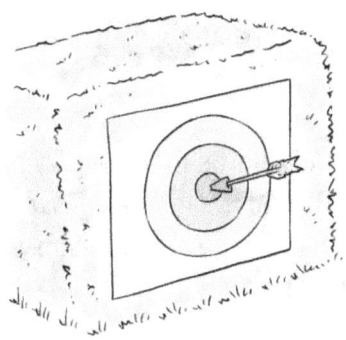

Once we have even the most basic market MAP, now we're ready to target where we think we can get the most bang for our sales buck. Targeting can be as simple as you take A-L, I'll take M-Z, or as sophisticated as you want to make it, including well planned out campaigns by calendar, season, geography, competitor, product vertical, special promotions etc.

What's the first step in targeting anything? Knowing how much ammunition you have.

If Pauly has 100 sauce sales people in Manhattan, he can do the whole freakin' village man. But Pauly doesn't have 100 sales people. Pauly has two sales people, Vinnie and Maria (We had to take care of Sal – he wasn't working out), because he knows he needs to grow his business, and because he spent 9.99 on this book, he knows he must have at least two, or not bother.

Manhattan has three major areas - Uptown, Downtown, and Midtown.

And the sauce buyers are fairly well distributed across all three areas.

Remember our MAP told us that there were 1000 buyers of sauce that we know in Manhattan. We're already doing business with 100 of them, so that means there are 900 that we can go after right now.

There's another 1000 that we don't know enough about to decide whether we should target them, so somebody should probably be trying to get that information while we're out pounding the pavement.

How many of those 900 can we go after in a year?

Well, we have 50 weeks in a year and we are pretty sure a sales person can engage with at least 3 new prospects per week while still taking care of existing customer needs that can't be handled by the shop. And in this business, engagement has to be a face to face meeting. No one is buying your sauce without tasting it and knowing who they are dealing with. Back when Pauly first started, he was able to meet with at least that many AND make his mama's famous sauce, so if he can do it, Vinnie and Maria can do it.

So we can engage with 300 prospects this year with our current sales team.

Maria is going to target the 150 biggest in Uptown because she lives up that way and that reduces her travel time considerably. Vinnie is going to target the 150 biggest in Midtown because he knows that market well from when he used to sell yellow page ads. That business isn't so hot anymore.

What about Downtown? Pauly doesn't have enough bandwidth to cover Downtown, so they aren't going to worry about it for now, but hopefully the new SELL·LEARN·REPEAT system will help them grow sales enough to afford at least one more rep.

And here's the good news for Pauly. They are going to make formal proposals to at least half those prospects (ergo 150 Proposals), and they are going to CLOSE every single one of those proposals.

I can feel Pauly getting bigger by the minute, can't you?

Don't even think that.

For more life changing insights on targeting, please refer to Chapter 20 on Ballard's 50/1 Rule.

TATER THOUGHTS

"Focus is a matter of deciding what things you're not going to do."

John Carmack

Chapter 11: ENGAGE

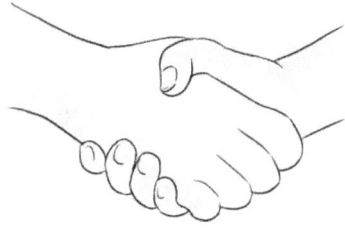

Most companies and sales people skip the first two steps and get right to this one. Who needs all them fancy databases and market maps - that all sounds like a bunch of hooey, or as my old grandpappy used to say, that's about as much good as a barrel of beaver balls.

Let's just jump on the A train and start knocking on doors, or better yet, just stroll down Broadway and scream "Who wants some f$%#in sauce!"

Incidentally, that would still be better than 95% of companies sales efforts because at least they got out of the office or the trade show and got to work.

After all, the money is in the street.

But Vinnie and Maria know better now and they have Pauly backing them up all the way. So they are ready to engage in a methodical, systematic fashion. They have their targets in a database and they plotted them all out in cloud based map tool they found for free so they can be efficient in planning their days.

So now Vinnie and Maria start knocking on doors, shaking hands, and meeting decision makers face to face, day in and day out, from sun up to sundown.

If you are really cut out for a career in sales, this is the fun part of the job - meeting new people and forging new relationships, many of which will last a lifetime.

No matter how developed your sales skills, if you can successfully engage your market and get them talking about their business, you can be great at sales. This IS the job.

And here's what you are trying to do with every engagement:

- Find out if this is the kind of company you want to do business with.
- Learn everything you can about their needs and how you can help them.
- Establish if there is a common interest in an ongoing business relationship.
- Get enough information and insight to provide an informed proposal.

Or, put another way, you need to get this far enough down the road to where they are genuinely interested in what you have to offer, and will seriously consider it.

If you can't get it that far, then learn what you can, update your MAP, and move on to prospects where you can.

That's all there is to it.

You need help developing rapport or starting a conversation or asking the right questions?

Those are different books, but I can tell you that your job is like CSI: SALES. You are a **C**USTOMER **S**ITUATION **I**NVESTIGATOR. Every opportunity leaves *some trace.*

I think today's best sales professionals are much more like seasoned detectives than they are wheelers and dealers.

Break out the luminol and latex and don't be afraid to use David Caruso cliches - whatever it takes.

One litmus test that you can use to decide when to move on from a prospect for the time being, is ask yourself honestly whether there is a two-way flow of information, or you just throwing spaghetti (and sauce) at their wall.

This is no different than romantic relationships. If they ain't returning any of your texts or calls, or never share any information with you, then they probably just aren't that into you. When you get this feeling, don't be afraid to politely, but directly ask the customer whether they are sincerely interested in considering what your company has to offer.

After all, you and your business deserve respect and consideration. If you don't act that way, don't expect the customer to treat you that way.

"Gentleman, when we find the beavers that match these balls, we'll find our perp."

TATER THOUGHTS

"You can't win every sale, but you can make sure you are meeting with decision makers that can buy your products or services more than your competition. Start with that."

Craig Ballard

Chapter 12:
PROPOSE

We have a MAP of our market. We TARGETED our top prospects. We ENGAGED those prospects and found some willing participants who were sincerely interested (or are really good at faking sincerity) in seeing a proposal from our company.

This is a very crucial step indeed and if we have done a good job of our investigation and we aren't in hot water with

Lieutenant Caine, then we should be in a position to provide an *informed* proposal that is framed to leverage our unique advantages.

And you know you have an informed proposal when you know that its better for your customer *in advance.* In other words, in most cases, you should already know that your proposal is a superior value to what they have today, even after factoring in their switching costs (The very real tangible and intangible costs they will experience from switching vendors).

Maria met with Pisano's owner Angelo. She learned a great deal about his business and the issues he has with his current sauce provider. Angelo has given Maria all his buying volumes for the last two years, and he's also told her roughly what he is paying now for his sauce. He is very interested in seeing what Maria can offer and is looking forward to her proposal.

Maria knows that Angelo doesn't like the fact that his current supplier only delivers on Friday's because that is his busiest day of the week and it's a hassle trying to have someone there to handle the delivery. If he wants it on a different day or runs out of stock before Friday, there's an extra delivery charge. He also doesn't like his payment terms, which are cash up front only, despite the fact he has an excellent reputation in the industry and great credit rating. Lastly, he feels the sauce is too expensive for the quality he is getting. He wouldn't mind paying a premium, but not for run of the mill sauce. Lastly, sometimes he overestimates his numbers and ends up buying too much sauce that he can't use, which ends up getting thrown out and that costs a lot of money.

He is worried that his customers are used to the old sauce, and it might take awhile before they fully embrace a different product - he's worried that could cost him sales.

Maria knows a lot about Angelo's business and she has a lot to work with in putting together a proposal that she knows will be a big improvement over what he has today.

Because she has done her homework and asked the hard questions, the proposal part is easy, and she didn't mind asking the questions because she is doing it to help Angelo. The more she knows, the better she can do for him. It's in her best interest to ask and it's in his best interest to answer. It's that simple.

So Maria's proposal looks something like this:

Proposal for Pisano's Pasta Parlour

> Product: Pauly's Perfect Red Pasta Sauce, Recipe 604
> Annual Volume: 700 barrels per year
> Price: $30 per barrel
> Terms: End of Month following Invoice
> Delivery: Prepaid minimum 5 barrels, Mon-Fri
> Loyalty Rebate: 5% rebate at end of first year if over 600 barrels
> New Sauce Promotion: No Risk - Sauce for Two Weeks

Maria knows this proposal not only meets all of Angelo's needs, but it is also framed to Pauly's advantages.

Pauly's sauce isn't cheaper than the competition, but he has a great reputation for quality ingredients, and Angelo can see and taste the difference. He won't reduce his product cost, but his value for his customers just went way up.

His payment flexibility and cash flow improved significantly.

He can get delivery when it's convenient for him, at no extra charge.

He gets a rebate of 5% at the end of the year for staying loyal to Pauly's - and that's a nice little stocking stuffer he wasn't counting on.

Lastly, he gets to try the sauce out of 2 weeks with his customers. If they don't love it, he doesn't have to pay for it - period, but Maria knows they will love it.

Maria knows it is a better deal than what Angelo has now because she did a thorough investigation during the engagement.

She also knows it is framed to leverage Pauly's unique advantages:

- Pauly's has excellent profitability, cash flow and cash management, so they can offer terms to the right customers - no problem.

- Pauly's has a truck on the road every day in Uptown because that's where most of their customers are now. Flexible delivery is no big deal if they hit the minimum order size, and even if they need an extra barrel here or there, no big deal.

- Pauly has the best sauce in town and his salespeople know it. They have no problem offering a no risk guarantee because they are 100% confident the customers will love it. They always do.

So, Maria did a fantastic job of providing an informed proposal, and one that she knows she has an excellent chance of winning.

This is the exact opposite of LAZY PRICE SHEET SELLING, which consists of running around dropping off price sheets (or emailing them) and then asking the customer to call you if they see anything interesting, or asking 'where do I need to be?'

If you want to do price sheet selling, hire a shaved monkey or buy a drone because you don't need professional sales people to drop off price sheets. If that's what your sales people are doing, then find new sales people. Don't worry, the old ones have a future in putting flyers under windshield wipers.

Now, here's the great news for Maria and Pauly.

No matter what happens now, she is going to CLOSE this opportunity.

TATER THOUGHTS

"If you have done the hard work, by the time you get to the proposal, you should truly believe that what you are proposing to the customer is clearly better value to their company than any alternative, including factoring in whatever switching costs may be involved."

Craig Ballard

TATER THOUGHTS

"Don't bolt your door with a boiled carrot."

Can't claim credit for this but I can tell you from actual experience, it is excellent advice.

Craig Ballard

Chapter 14:
CLOSE

Hey, did you notice there's no 13th Chapter? Its just like hotels with no 13th floor. I learned as an adult that they didn't actually skip an entire floor and leave it empty. I used to freak out when I was a kid thinking what would happen if I accidentally got stranded on the 13th floor, which doesn't exist, and cannot be reached by elevator. Worse yet, no room service. I digress.

In this case, it isn't because of silly superstition, it's because I want to jog your brain to pay even more attention to this oh so critical step.

Without this step, everything else has been an enormous waste of both or time, but especially mine.

When we CLOSE, yes - we are trying to win the business. We are going to ask for the business. We are going to use every technique known to man and Zig Zigler to get the customer to say yes, but even if we don't win, we are still going to CLOSE, because you are now going to **change your definition of CLOSING forever**.

TO CLOSE an opportunity is to get a definitive FINAL answer (YES, NO) on your proposal and to <u>LEARN</u> the most important reasons behind that final outcome.

Because the single most important and sacred task of the salesperson in the SELL-LEARN-REPEAT process is to gain insights that can help the salesperson and their organization refine and improve and their value proposition and gain competitive advantage.

And here's the most beautiful fact that should change your life forever.

You cannot LOSE on an opportunity if you learn something valuable that can help your business the next time around.

The only way you can lose with SELL·LEARN·REPEAT **is if you don't learn**.

And so this is the mission of all SELL·LEARN·REPEAT soldiers. Yes, they want to win, but whether they win this time or not, they must LEARN.

Let's check back with Maria and see how she makes out with Angelo. No there will be no french kissing involved - take it easy.

Maria is ready to close. She is confident in her proposal. She has a good feeling from Angelo - he really seems excited about the prospect of working with Pauly's.

So, she meets with Angelo at is restaurant and asks Angelo a simple question, 'Can we do business together?'

And Angelo's response.

Absolutely Maria. I really liked your proposal - it addressed all my concerns and I think it's going to be a great relationship. I can't wait until our customers taste the new sauce.

Maria is thrilled, but she hasn't closed this opportunity.

And if you have been actually comprehending what you are reading, then you already know why.

The opportunity isn't closed, win or lose, until we LEARN from it.

So, Maria responds:

'Angelo, thank you - that is fantastic news and I'm so excited to have you as our business partner. Let's get your new account set up today and our team will get to work on that first order.

I do have one really important question I need to ask. **In our company, learning is even more important than winning.**

I know there was a lot of factors that went into this decision, but what is the single most important reason you chose to do business with our company?'

Angelo, paused for a second and furrowed his brow.

'That's a great question Maria - no one has ever asked me that before. Well, you're right, there was a lot of reasons, but if I had to choose the single most important one, it would have to be the taste. Your sauce is so fresh and rich and even though it's a little bit higher price, I think it's going to bring more customers in our door and keep then coming back.'

Now Maria can write her CLOSE Report, and be sure to select the proper category for the PRIMARY REASON.

This is incredibly valuable information, and the more she collects, the smarter her and Pauly's will get about how their value proposition is playing in the market place, and whether they win or not, how they can improve it.

Just because Maria won this account, doesn't mean there is nothing to be learned.

If Angelo had said that a better price was the determining factor, that may not necessarily be good news for Pauly's, because they want to position themselves as the premium product in the market and don't want to predominantly win on price - that could mean they are leaving money on the table.

Now, lets say it went a different way. Maybe Angelo had a different response:

"Maria, you provided a really great proposal, and I have to admit, it really is better than what we have today in every respect. But my second cousin is the sales guy for the sauce we use now and we go way back, and I just don't think I can change right now. I really appreciate all your efforts.'

Well, Maria is mad at herself for not uncovering this earlier in her investigation, but at least she got a final answer and learned something incredibly important about this account.

As long as Angelo's cousin is in the sauce business, he ain't changing to Pauly's.

Maria still closed the opportunity, and she completed her Closing Report.

Now this tree is tagged so that no one spends a lot of time taking the ax to it the future, other than to find out if Angelo's cousin is still in the sauce business, so Maria will check in every 6 months or so just to see how Angelo is doing, and who knows, maybe his cousin will have an unfortunate shaving accident. Life is funny like that.

Note 1: That's a joke - I am not advocating whacking[2] your competition.
Note 2: I'm not advocating whacking anything[3].
Note 3: Not that there's anything wrong with that.

Win or Lose, Maria has CLOSED and done the job she is getting paid to do. Maria and most other sales people won't win most of the time, but the difference between Maria and most other sales people is that she CLOSES every single time she PROPOSES and we just turned our sales force into a BIG DATA machine.

Can you say the same?

REPEAT AFTER ME:

THE ONLY WAY YOU LOSE ANY SALE IS IF YOU DON'T LEARN SOMETHING VALUABLE

TATER THOUGHTS

"The only way you will ever lose another sale is if your company can't learn from it.

Closing the deal means win or lose, getting a definitive answer on your proposal including the most important reasons why you did or didn't win the business."

Craig Ballard

Chapter 15: ADAPT

The point of collecting the incredible data that our top investigators like Maria are collecting every day is to use it to get better.

And yes, its a cliche, but its also true - the world changes faster now. Information is ubiquitous and real time.

You have to constantly review what you are learning from the market and interpret what it means for your business, and decide how best to use it to your advantage.

And you need to ADAPT when things are going bad, and also when they are going good.

If you think the world is terrible and everything is going to shit, just wait.

And…

If you think the world is magnificent and you have the world by the tail, just wait.

Things change. Ask Blockbuster, Polaroid, Myspace, Blackberry, and Macdonald's and the list goes on, about how things can change like *that.*

Complacency will be your undoing. If you don't continuously learn and improve as a person or a company, you will be made obsolete, and probably sooner than later.

But, you have a MASSIVE advantage because you paid $9.99 for this book.

You have a FEEDBACK LOOP that gives you the leg up on the competition. They are too dumb or lazy or both to use this kind of disciplined process. They are out their flinging prices sheets like dolla bills yo, but you are smarter - you know the game is about learning, and if you are learning, you will be winning eventually.

Pauly's is a SELL·LEARN·REPEAT disciple, and so are all their salespeople. They believe in things like databases and measurement and accountability, and they always CLOSE on their proposals, so they have some really valuable information about their sales resources and their market. Not to mention, their MAP just keeps getting better and better.

Pauly got Franky in the back office to put together a couple key reports from all of the Closing Reports submitted by Maria and Vinnie, plus the two new reps they added because their sales growth has been so strong. They now cover Downtown and Brooklyn. Franky does these reports at the end of every month, but here's the year end summaries - this is where all that rubber hits the road.

All the sales reps' hard work in the streets has culminated in these table. Of course the data could be further sliced and diced for a variety of purposes and we can drill down into any level of detail we want, including the specifics of each opportunity, but let's keep it simple for now to demonstrate the concept. I'm here to give you scaffolding, not the Sistine Chapel.

Pauly's Sales Productivity Summary - FY16

Rep	Territory	ENGAGE	CLOSE	CLOSE %	WIN	WIN %	Estimated Annual Revenue	Realized Revenue Last 12
Vinnie	Midtown	140	63	45%	26	41%	$598,000	$119,600
Maria	Uptown	160	80	50%	32	40%	$416,000	$208,000
Angelina	Downtown	180	92	51%	46	50%	$1,058,000	$423,200
Rocco	Brooklyn	100	40	40%	6	15%	$400,000	$80,000
Total		580	275	47%	110	40%	$2,472,000	$830,800

This productivity report shows us how effective our sales investments are performing overall and gives us a good indication of relative performance amongst the players on the team. We can use this data to adapt our strategy, provide constructive feedback or guidance, or potentially make changes to the team.

What conclusions could we draw from this report?

Firstly, Angelina has been our strongest sales rep by a considerable margin. She engages more, she closes more, and she wins more of her closes.

Maria is our next strongest resource, although generated about half of what Angelina produced during the year. Still, very solid.

Vinnie is doing ok, but he fell short of his minimum CLOSE target of 75 Closes and he tends to exaggerate his estimated annual revenues from new sales.

Rocco struggled, and didn't even come close to hitting his CLOSE target, so he forfeited much of his bonus pay, and his winning percentage on Closes was the lowest on the team, as was his revenue generated.

Pauly has to ask himself if Rocco is someone that he should continue to invest in, or if perhaps he just isn't cut out for this job. If he had hit his CLOSE target, he would have done much better, so maybe it's a coaching opportunity, where he can plan his time more efficiently and also improve his skills when it comes to winning the business.

Even with two salespeople, at least you have some frame of reference for what is possible. The more people you have on your team, the more rich and accurate the data becomes, where you can quickly identify who is kicking ass and chewing bubble gum and who is struggling.

All the sales people should be reading Angelina's closing reports to get insights into what she may be doing differently to win more business.

Pauly should be reviewing everyone's closing reports at least weekly, especially Rocco's to see where they may be losing their way, or leaving money on the table.

Before we move on, let's whip back to Ballard's Rule of 2, and see why it is SO important to have more than one salesperson, because here's what Pauly's sales productivity report looked like before he brought on more resources.

Rep	Territory	ENGAGE	CLOSE	CLOSE %	WIN	WIN %	Estimated Annual Revenue	Realized Revenue Last 12
Vinnie	Midtown	140	63	45%	26	41%	$598,000	$119,600

Is this good or bad? It's impossible to know because we have nothing to compare it to.

We can only look at it in a very narrow sense in terms of whether it is a good use of funds for the business, but we don't know if much better outcomes possible.

If Gross Profit Margin on Vinnie's sales is 30%, then he generated about 36K in growth in gross profit during the year, assuming he maintained the base of existing customers, and about 72K in recurring gross profit on an annual basis.[14]

Vinnie's cost, including his employment taxes, benefits, and his car is about 60K, so you could say he paid for himself, which is usually **what I consider the minimum standard** for sales people whose primary purpose is to grow the business.

Ultimately, Pauly found out that Vinnie is towards the bottom end of the pack in terms of sales productivity, and he knows that there are people who can generate 2-4 times as much as him, for about the same price.

Pauly's Market Intel Summary - FY16

---

[14] Why 72K? Because 36K was what was generated throughout the year, but half those customers only generated revenue for half a year or less, so once all those customers are steady state for a year, they would generate 72K per year. More on this in Chapter 18. Trust me, I'm right, again.

Primary Reason	WIN		LOSE		Win %	Lose %
	Count	%	Count	%		
Products Features & Benefits	55	50%	12	7%	82%	18%
Price	13	12%	51	28%	20%	80%
Relationship	12	11%	31	17%	28%	72%
Service	18	16%	8	4%	69%	31%
Brand	6	5%	35	20%	15%	85%
Payment Terms	6	5%	3	2%	67%	33%
Saticficed	0	0%	39	22%	0%	100%
Total CLOSED	110	100%	179	100%	38%	62%

What can we learn from this market focused view of the data?

Well, we know we win 32% of the proposals we close. We also know that the number one reason we win is products features and benefits - our sauce is awesome.

In fact, when we are competing primarily on the quality of our sauce, we win over 75% of the time.

The number one reason we lose is on price, and we lose 3 out of 4 battles on that front.

That's not necessarily a bad thing, because we don't want to be the low cost provider, as long as we are winning our fair share overall and are winning where we want to have the advantage.

The Relationship numbers are concerning because those can be tougher nuts to crack. That may be an indication of our time and experience in the market or that there are established players that have deep roots and relationships with customers.

The brand numbers are also of interest, because Pauly's feels his sauce is the best, and they need to spend more money, time, and effort on building their brand awareness in the marketplace.

Lastly, the Satisficed figures signal a potential opportunity.

Pauly's lost 39 times because the customer was Satisficed. That means he acknowledges the proposal was at least a little better than what he had, but that he was just too comfortable in his old shoes to make a change.

This is another way of saying that the proposal addressed all his direct costs and value concerns, but didn't adequately address the cost of switching suppliers.

So, the sales team perhaps didn't do as much as they should have to get that willing prospect off the fence, or they didn't adequately compensate for the switching costs in their proposal.

The good news is, these are the ones that are often easiest to take a second crack at, by sweetening the deal or reducing the risks and hassle to the customer.

I don't like to see Satisficed figures in the double digits. That tells me we had a live one on the line that wanted to business with my company and we let it get away.

Pauly needs to work with the sales team on some new tools they can use when they go back into the market (and to those prospects who we already know like our proposal) that can address switching costs, such as:

1. Marketing incentives or allowances to address the risk of changing an established brand.
2. Risk free trial periods, money back guarantees, if you don't love it after 30 days etc.
3. Purchase of existing inventories or equipment connect to existing supplier.
4. Investment in new fixtures or signage to address any upfront expenditures they may have.
5. One time implementation rebates to address their time, effort, and hassle, associated with switching to your company.

Bottom line: Ignore switching costs in your proposals at your peril. The initial cost of overcoming them is usually a fraction of the cost of not winning the business.

Alright, you know how to use the data you learned from CLOSING to ADAPT your business in the most powerful ways, from the productivity of your sales team to the effectiveness of your value proposition in the market.

Of course, we just scratched the surface of how many ways we can use the CLOSING data to build lasting competitive advantage, and I'm sure you are already thinking of 100 more ways you can take advantage of me.

We have come full circle. You have finished your first SELL·LEARN·REPEAT revolution, and this is the fundamental building block of your sales growth revolution.

You should be full of beans and ready to change the world.

You have everything you need right now to grow your sales by double digits every single year.

A simple thank you would suffice.

We're not really all done. I like my customers to get a little more than they expected.

That's why I included Part 3. I want you to finish this book and think, that's the best damn $9.99 I ever spent in my life, other than buying the first season of Game of Thrones.

That's a given.

TATER THOUGHTS

"Every success story is a tale of constant adaption, revision and change."

Richard Branson

Chapter 16:
REPEAT, REPEAT, REPEAT...REPEAT, AGAIN

At the risk of repeating myself, you don't wake up and smell the SELL·LEARN·REPEAT coffee once. You wake up every day and smell the SELL·LEARN·REPEAT. In fact, every time you wake up I want you to chant like a demon:

MAP, TARGET, ENGAGE, PROPOSE, CLOSE, ADAPT + REPEAT

and again,

MAP, TARGET, ENGAGE, PROPOSE, CLOSE, ADAPT + REPEAT

The POWER OF SELL·LEARN·REPEAT COMPELS YOU!

SELL·LEARN·REPEAT is a feedback LOOP. A loop is something that goes AROUND and AROUND (queue RATT, yes I did)

As you complete this process over and over - hundreds and thousands of times throughout months and years, your MAP should get more rich, accurate, and complete. It will become a competitive advantage for your business. NO ONE will know more about your market than YOU - not even close.

Your targeting will get smarter. Your engagements will be more focused and powerful.

Your proposals will be better suited the needs of your customers and get more leverage from your unique advantages.

You will win more of your CLOSES.

You will ADAPT and learn faster than your competitors.

The value of the SELL·LEARN·REPEAT sales growth system gets exponentially higher the more you use it. It is your sales growth brain getting bigger, smarter and faster after every cycle.

The more you use the machine, the stronger the machine gets. The bigger your data gets, the more valuable the data becomes.

TATER THOUGHTS

"Discipline is the soul of an army. It makes small numbers formidable; procures success to the weak, and esteem to all."

George Washington

Part 3 – Really Advanced Concepts

Chapter 17: Revenue is Overrated

That's right, you heard me.

You need to stop worrying about 'hitting your numbers'. When a farmer needs corn, does he go into a barren field and scream "GROW!"?

No, he doesn't. To grow corn you need to plant seeds (and pay Monsanto a royalty, because I think they own the DNA for corn), so if he is trying to hit his crop yield numbers come harvest, he's going to have to plant enough seeds and get them enough water.

Do you scream at your own stomach - "Hey, we're going to be shirtless at the beach on Saturday - I need to see at least two distinguishable abs"!

Nope. If you need abs in three days, then screaming ain't going to help. Vomiting for 72 hours straight – possibly, but not recommended.

Revenue doesn't happen out of thin air - **it is the ends, not the means**. It is very difficult to control *in the short term,* so stop wasting your time trying. You'll just get everybody all worked up like a bunch of floured ferrets in a frying pan, as my old grandpappy used to say.

For SELL·LEARN·REPEAT disciples, revenue is absolutely controllable in the long term, as long as you focus on the right things NOW.

In the short term, you need to focus on the things that are entirely within your control.

You have complete control over how many engagements and closes you do NEXT QUARTER, and next year, and the year after that.

It is entirely predictable.

And you cannot get new sales without new CLOSES, so if I were you, I would start worrying more about hitting your CLOSE numbers, and less about revenue.

In other words, focus on the inputs, not the outputs. Focus on planting the seeds, and doing the crunches - these things are entirely within your control. (But don't eat the corn if you want abs - that's a simple carb full of sugar, sorry).

If you are following the SELL·LEARN·REPEAT process, then you are creating future revenue, every revolution.

Eventually, you will have so much data from this process, that you can PREDICT your organic revenue growth within a few percentage points.

And the more you follow the process, the better your growth machine will work.

The next time anyone asks you how the numbers look, tell them they look exactly as we planned them.

Tell them the numbers are exactly as we agreed on for this period.

Imagine that.

"Damnit, I need everybody to run around like horny wildebeests to hit the numbers this month because I don't know how to make revenue growth a process!"

TATER THOUGHTS

"When you shift your culture to one where sales growth is a repeatable process, revenue will become a predictable output. You can't control revenue in the short term, so focus on the things you can control now that will lead to revenue in the future."

Craig Ballard

Chapter 18: Build Sales Growth & ROI Metrics

Our CLOSE reports and database will very quickly start to give us valuable information we can use to make our sales growth far more predictable, and the more data we collect, the more accurate our predictions will be.

Recall in the last chapter (that was like one chapter ago) that we agreed revenue is overrated and not the primary focus of SELL-LEARN-REPEAT disciple.

What we are far more interested in is in establishing metrics for our sales growth, which is to say, what are the expected outputs (revenue - something we can't directly control) from our planned inputs (CLOSES) - something we have a great deal of control over.

Remember our trusty Sales Productivity report from Pauly's?

CLOSER	Territory	ENGAGE	CLOSE	CLOSE %	WIN	WIN %	Estimated Annual Revenue	Realized Revenue Last 12
Vinnie	Midtown	140	63	45%	26	41%	$598,000	$119,600
Maria	Uptown	160	80	50%	32	40%	$416,000	$208,000
Angelina	Downtown	180	92	51%	46	50%	$1,058,000	$423,200
Rocco	Brooklyn	100	40	40%	6	15%	$400,000	$80,000
Total		580	275	47%	110	40%	$2,472,000	$830,800
	PER CLOSER	145	68.75				PER CLOSE	$3021

This report tells us that on average, we can expect $3021 in realized revenue (actually billed during the year) per CLOSE during that year.

Not $3021 per WIN, but $3021 per CLOSE, on average. You with me?

So, if we want to grow the business by at least $2M the following year, how many CLOSES do we need?

There's a conservative calculation and an optimistic calculation.

Conservatively, to achieve $1.5M in sales growth, Pauly's will need:

$2,000,000 ÷ $3012 = **664 CLOSES**

Why is this conservative?

Well, remember our realized revenue was based on what we actually billed from the CLOSED customers throughout the year.

And, if we just make it simple and assume those customers were added throughout the year, then I didn't realize the full annual revenue potential of all those customers.

The customers I added in the first month will generate revenue for 12 months in that year, but the customer I added in the 11th month only generated revenue for 1 month.

Let me spare you the math and just tell you that in theory, assuming an equal distribution of customers being added through the year and an even distribution of the size of customer, then the realized revenue in that year should be about half the full annual revenue that those customers will generate.

Here's what that looks like visually. As opposed to what it looks like orally.

Figure 3: New Customer Revenue Ramps up to Steady State

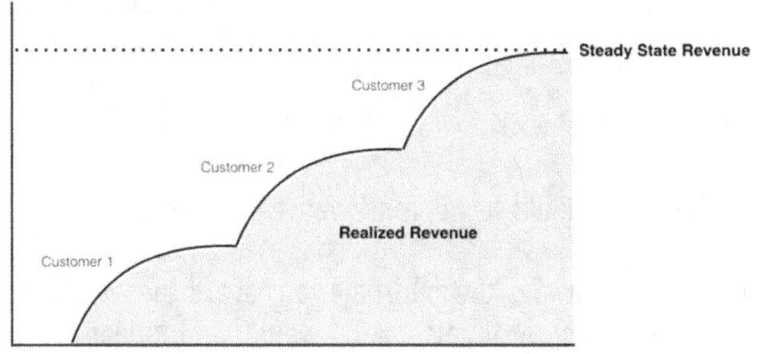

So, 664 CLOSES is conservative for generating $2.0M in new revenue because it assumes I won't get the other half of the revenue from customers I added last year. All of it will have to come from new opportunities.

You with me? Good.

Now, if we want to be optimistic, and assume our realized revenue is indeed half of what we will achieve for those customers for a full year of sales, then we should also be seeing that other half this coming year.

So, how do I get to $2.0M in sales growth if I am being optimistic?

Some of the $2.0M is already in the bank right?

$2,000,000 - (275 X $3021 = $830,800) = $1,169,200

So, I'm going to need another $1.17M in new sales revenue on top of the 830K that was growth in the bank from last year.

$1,169,200 ÷ $3012 = **388 CLOSES**

Which way should we go, conservative or optimistic?

The short answer is, the more data you have, the less variability and risk in your estimates. So, I would tend to lean toward conservative estimates in the my first couple years of SELL·LEARN·REPEAT. After I have established more solid trends from hundreds and thousands of data points and validated realized revenue from CLOSES, you can err on the optimistic side, which is no longer really optimistic - just well informed.

Pauly and Franky decide to err on the conservative side since they have only being using the SELL·LEARN·REPEAT process for one full year, and they go with 450 CLOSES for next year. Worst case, this should generate about $1.35M in sales growth next year. Best case, over $2.15M in sales growth.

But how many CLOSERS will they need to accomplish this goal, and what will that cost?

Will this be a good investment for Pauly's?

My sales productivity data tells me my CLOSERS should each accomplish a minimum of 70 CLOSES per year (if Angelina can do 92, then everyone is going to do at least 70 and Rocco and Vinnie are going to have to pick up their socks or they will be sleeping with the fishes[15]), so I will need at least 7 CLOSERS to reach my goal of 450.

That's 3 more CLOSERS than I have today, and they won't all be CLOSING on their first day, so we need to get hiring right away.

But wait a second, can Pauly's afford it? Is it a good ROI for Pauly's business?

Here's how us SELL·LEARN·REPEAT types do that analysis:

CLOSERS	AVG Fully Loaded Cost	Total Cost	CLOSES PER CLOSER	Recurring Annual Revenue per Close	Gross Profit Margin	Recurring Annual GP	Sales Investment Multiple
7	$85,000	$595,000	70	$6024	$1807	$885,528	1.5

So, think about if we were going to invest 595K into a business. Would we be pretty happy if that business generated 885K in gross profit margin in its first year?

Most companies would pay at least 1X the bottom line of a business, especially one where they felt confident in the repeatability of that bottom line.

In this case, we will generate 1.5X our initial investment in recurring annual gross profit, so that's even better.

What's the right investment criteria or Sales Investment Multiple?

---

[15] Which is an industry term for having to sell wholesale tuna.

I'm not going to cop out and say you have to buy my next book to find out, but this isn't a black and white question. In fact race has nothing to do with it.

As a rule of thumb, I say if you can cover the cost of your sales investment with the growth in recurring gross profit it generates (after all direct cost of sales), then that's a very good bet for most businesses and one you will be glad you made.

Companies that profitably grow their revenues faster than their competitors typically become the leaders in their industry. And Pauly's will be the 300 LB gorilla in New York sauce if he sticks to the system.

At some point, as his market share increases, will those $ per close go down?

If he doesn't add new products or territories, probably yes - because it will get harder to grow revenues the more market share you get (especially beyond 50%), but let's face it, that's a great problem to have, and Pauly, like most folks has a long way to go before he starts hitting any walls.

And there's a lot of things Pauly can do before he ever gets close to that wall. Heck, he hasn't even stepped foot in Jersey yet.

OK, what have we learned?

Well, if you follow the SELL·LEARN·REPEAT process, sales growth will quickly become reliable and predictable.

You will build sales growth metrics that will allow you to plan the growth for your business, and to determine if that represents a good return on your investment, whether you have 2 CLOSERS or 2000 - the same process and principals apply.

- What is your sales growth target
- How much sales growth can you generate per CLOSE
- How many CLOSES will it take to get there
- How many CLOSERS will you need
- Does the Sales Investment Multiple make sense for your business?
- Get on with it.

Revenue growth and financial targets will no longer be crystal ball territory for you or your business.

You will no longer slam your fist and tell you sales people to hit their numbers.

You will be a quiet, stone cold sales growth gangster that gets smarter every CLOSE you make.

Queue slow clap and credits.

You have everything you need right now to change the future for you and your company - forever, and you didn't have to pay a 22 year old with skinny jeans from McKinsey $700K to do a SWOT analysis.

You're welcome, but we're not quite done. Its time for one final slap upside the head in Chapter 19, because like my old Grandpappy used to say, never try to feed a squirrel while you are standing on his nuts[16].

---

[16] Ok, that one's hazy - I'm paraphrasing. Never trust a squirrel that can't find his own nuts...no, that's not it either. I remembered most of them, cut me some slack.

TATER THOUGHTS

"If you can't measure it, you can't improve it."

Peter Drucker

Chapter 19:
Hunters & Huggers

We've all heard it before when talking about sales people – is this guy or gal a hunter or a farmer?

Are they a stone code killer, or a glorified order filler?

True hunters are thought of as the big time closers. The guys who can break down an ice cold door and extract a PO before the buyer knows what hits them. They're like the bad cop in the interrogation room. Hyper-aggressive and seething with testosterone. Hunters love the hunt and the kill above all else – they are often on to the next deal while the carcass is still warm.

But farmers feed the village too – they just do it in a different way. Once you have a customer in your camp, you can still grow the business you do together over time and this is often the fastest and most overlooked way to grow revenues.

It also depends on whether you are an upstart company trying to scratch and claw your way up from the bottom or an established leader with substantial market share.

If the hunters have killed most of the buffalo, then you better start getting good at farming.

If you need to attack the market with shock and awe and bring fresh meat home to the village, then a bunch of guys in overalls with pitchforks ain't going to be much help.

But whether you are hunting or farming, as long as you have opportunities to grow your business and are CLOSING as per the SELL·LEARN·REPEAT method, then you can get consistently great results from a broad range of skill sets and personality types.

So, I want to set the record straight and say farming isn't a dirty word – farming has its place in the SELL·LEARN·REPEAT world, but new business opportunities with existing customers have to be CLOSED just the same as any other prospect.

You have to learn from every type of opportunity and you have to pursue each with **the same process and discipline.**

There are different types of detectives and different types of sales people.

Some are larger than life and everybody's instant best friend. Some are more quiet and observing and think before they speak, but that doesn't mean they are any less competitive or effective.

As long as they are intellectually curious by nature, can work with a database (CRM), are committed to engaging the market at a high pace, doing their homework, asking the right questions, preparing an informed proposal, and getting a definitive answer to that proposal – then they will CLOSE every time, and all but the most socially or deodorant challenged will get their fair share of wins.

There is one specific type you will want to watch out for in the SELL·LEARN·REPEAT world.

BEWARE THE HUGGER

These are the 'sales' people that prefer to be in very safe and controlled selling environments where their customers and transactions are well defined and predictable. They are often afraid to ask even basic questions or push for answers and don't like to be thrown in front of new people and situations on a regular basis. They will not survive outside captivity.

Professional Account Huggers (or PAH's for short) never stray too far from the people or products they know well. They bring doughnuts and Christmas calendars and occasionally take orders if cornered, but they don't CLOSE. Huggers are lousy detectives.

The right combination of hunting and farming ensures the village has a healthy diet of growth. Leave the Huggers for Hallmark.

TATER THOUGHTS

The Scorpion and the Frog

 A scorpion and a frog meet on the bank of a stream and the scorpion asks the frog to carry him across on its back. The frog asks, "How do I know you won't sting me?" The scorpion says, "Because if I do, I will die too."

The frog is satisfied, and they set out, but in midstream, the scorpion stings the frog. The frog feels the onset of paralysis and starts to sink, knowing they both will drown, but has just enough time to gasp "Why?"

Replies the scorpion: "It's in my nature..."

What does this have to do with sales growth?

If you ask a Hugger or Farmer to be a Hunter, you will be disappointed. Hunters will grow bored and frustrated with too much hugging and farming. Farmers and Huggers will be stressed beyond their limits if they are asked to pound the pavement and find new customers. The good news is everyone can follow processes – so match the needs of your organization with the nature and personality of your sales resources.

Chapter 20: Ballard's 50/1 Rule

I'm sure many people are familiar with the 80/20 rule which loosely translated means that 80% of outputs or effects are related to just 20% of the inputs or causes. 20% of the world's population create 80% of the world's pollution, 20% of a company's products generate 80% of its sales, 80% of the fun you'll have in your life occurred in your 20's, 20% of Donald Trump's hair covers 80% of his head – you get the idea.

This geezer Pareto claims to have come up with the idea or 'law' and his estate gets huge royalties from the whole thing. I grew up with Donny Pareto Jr. and he drove a Delorean to school, and he was 10. Anytime someone invokes the 80/20 rule, they get a piece. In fact, over 80% of the royalties are generated by 20% of the users, mostly consultants, who have to pay double for gratuitous overuse.

In all seriousness, its time for a new rule designed for our increasingly attention span deficient society who want everything faster and easier, and its called Ballard's 50/1 rule which states that 50% of the outputs will be related to 1% of the inputs. Let that blow your mind for a second.

I have mad respect for Pareto, but he simply didn't go far enough. He left money on the table and I'm not too proud to pick it up.

Let me break this down for you, nice and easy.

If you can get 80% of the value from 20% of the effort, then you must be able to get 64% of the output from 4% of the effort.

And if you can get 64% of the value from 4% of the effort, then you must be able to get about 50% of the value from less than 1% of the effort, but let's just call it the 50/1 rule.

I'll slow it down further for Geography majors:

20% = 80%

20% * 20% = 80% X 80%

Therefore 4% = 64%

20% * 4% = 80% X 64%

Therefore 0.8% = 51.2%, or 1% = 50% for short.

Think about that for a second. Would you want to be the guy or girl or spending a MONTH to make $10000 or would you rather spend 1 DAY to make $5000?

Do you want to 'focus' on 20% of the market with 80% of the sales, or 1% of the market with HALF the sales?

It isn't about being lazy, its about choosing your battles and getting the most bang for you buck.

When it comes to targeting and focus in sales, this is an incredibly important concept, and you're going to see The Ballard's 50/1 rule in almost every business and market, especially when you are the up and comer. Now – if you have 70% market share, then sure, you're going to have to go old school Pareto and eek out that last 10%, and its going to be tough.

If you aren't the dominant player in the market, or the market is fragmented, then Pareto is like taking a beaver to a bear fight[17], which generally doesn't end well.

Always start with the 1 that gets you 50 before you work on the 19 that gets you the next 30.

---

[17] Ironically, it is common knowledge in Canada that in a street fight, 1 Bear can handle about 50 Beavers at a time. If they are rabid beavers, then everyone knows all bets are off.

Ballard's 50/1 Rule

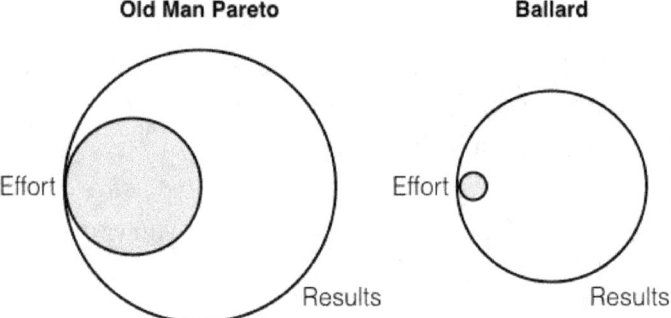

TATER THOUGHTS

"When it comes to setting priorities, start with 50/1 before you worry about 80/20. Find that one thing that can drive 50% of the results, then move to the 19 things that can get you the next 30%."

Craig Ballard

Chapter 21: Ballard's 3rd Law of Diminishing Chart Returns

Before you get too far down the road in your sales revolution, remember that Ballard's 3rd Law states that there is a diminishing marginal value in the usefulness of a chart or table to convey meaningful information or improve understanding of any concept for every object added to the chart.

There is an inflection point where added objects actually contribute negative value and reduce the overall value of the chart. My in depth studies with primates has shown that at approximately 25 objects per 8.5 x 11 page, the brain will experience information overload and in scientific terms, say WTF?

In fact, when shown charts from a prestigious consulting company that shall go unnamed, for charts with an object count exceeding 25, there was a marked increase in poo flinging behavior. A similar fecal distribution anomaly can be observed as the number of intersection points in a chart increases beyond five. If there are more than 25 objects and 5 or more intersections on a single chart, the brain is at risk of exploding, which makes cleaning up monkey poo a cakewalk in comparison. Curiously, some of the blank sheets used for experiment control in the study that were inadvertently hit by flying poo appeared in many cases to result in better charts than those used from professional sources.

Conversely, consider the essence of one of the most simple yet powerful process charts ever created:

Buy Low -> Sell High

or the incomparable

No Tickie -> No Laundry

Figure 4: Ballard's 3rd Law

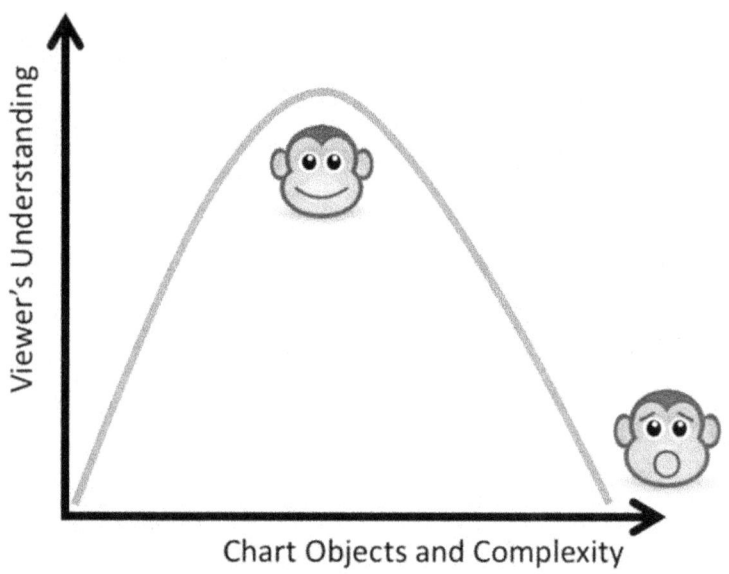

TATER THOUGHTS

"Any fool can make something complicated. It takes a genius to make it simple."

Woody Guthrie

Chapter 22: Ballard's 4th Law of Really Good Guys & Gals

Suffering from RGGS or Really Good Guy Syndrome? When you hear "What he/she does can't really be measured", what they really mean is that they don't really know what that person does or they aren't comfortable holding them accountable for producing any quantifiable results.

That doesn't necessarily mean they don't produce any quantifiable value, just that nobody really knows for sure. "Gee, I can't really point to one thing, but they are a REALLY good guy!". In my experience, that's probably NAGT "Not A Good Thing" if you are into 'ROI'.

The good news is that if what RGG's do can't really be measured, you know – in those traditional ways of 'measuring' things in business like 'how does this make money for the company and how much does it make', then if you lose them, you won't ever really know what you might have lost, because you won't be able to measure that either.

Sleep soundly knowing that Ballard's 4th Law is absolute: The important things you can measure (revenue, profits, ROI, etc), by pure Spock logic, can't possibly be adversely affected by removing something that can't!

Is there a sure fire shortcut to finding out if you may be suffering from RGGS? Absolutely. Either give your suspected RGG a one month vacation for all that great stuff they do, whatever you call that, or simply don't communicate with them for one month.

If you don't notice anything being different after a month, or no customers or other employees raise any red flags, then chances are you are suffering from RGGS.

Curing RGGS is especially tough because it requires an embarrassing conversation with someone who may feel insulted and hurt that you expect the same things of them as anyone else in the organization.

After all, they did help you move that time.

TATER THOUGHTS

"If you are worried about letting someone go because what they do for the company can't be measured, either start measuring or stop worrying."

Chapter 23.
That Sugar Won't Fly Anymore

I don't really mean sugar, but since I have leaned heavily on coffee metaphors, I figured I'd really milk it. Oops, there I go again.

Sugar, shit, whatever - it won't fly in a SELL·LEARN·REPEAT world and I don't take either in my coffee, organic or otherwise.

The cat is officially out of the bag. And if you have ever gotten a cat forcefully out of a bag, I can tell you from personal experience, it ain't ever going back in.

Organic sales growth isn't magic tribal knowledge passed down from generations or bestowed upon silver tongued backslappers at tradeshows.

Sales growth is a 6 step process that anyone can learn and implement, as long as they are committed to putting in the dedication and discipline needed to make it work.

- If you are a SELL·LEARN·REPEAT disciple, then every single one of your sales people is a CLOSER.

- If you are a SELL·LEARN·REPEAT disciple, then your sales growth is reliable and predictable.

- If you are a SELL·LEARN·REPEAT disciple, then your business gets stronger on every single CLOSE, win or lose.

- If you are a SELL·LEARN·REPEAT disciple, then you will kick the sugar out of your competition.

Sorry, there are no overpaid Sales Managers with SELL·LEARN·REPEAT, but we do have other Sales M positions for people that are detail oriented and are really good at organizing and managing processes and drawing insights from data.

If you don't think databases (fancy word for CRM) that collect, share, and report the most important information about your sales activity are critical to the success of the business, then we would like you to work for our competitor as soon as possible.

There is never EVER just one salesperson for any important product, channel or territory.

There is NEVER a time that I come into your office and you can't give me a report in 3 minutes (I'm not even giving you extra PC time - its 2016) that tells me everything I need to know about your market, sales productivity and ROI and how the market is responding to your value proposition in REAL TIME.

Welcome to no-excuseville, population YOU.

TATER THOUGHTS

"An excuse is worse and more terrible than a lie; for an excuse is a lie guarded."

Alexander Pope

Chapter 24:
For Serious Cases Only

Its funny - companies of all sizes will pay big money to consultants (including me, thankfully) to tell them how to improve their business in all sorts of ways - branding, ERPs, strategy, purchasing, operational efficiency, HR, etc. I have consulted on many of these things, and some of the projects were really important, but none of them were game changing. And very few of them were concerning the most difficult challenge facing the business.

The vast majority of consultants don't know a thing about sales growth, which is the single biggest determinant of survival and leadership in most industries today.

Traditional sales gurus can whip a room into a frenzy on closing the deal, but they themselves aren't process minded data junkies for the most part.

Certainly very few have ever led the systematic growth of any actual company in the real world.

There's a world of difference between knowing what to do and actually doing it.

If you want to pay for all those fancy reports and SWOT analysis or motivational seminars, you are going to have to sell something. That is where everything starts and ends for almost every business in the world.

The answers you seek are in these pages, so read it again before you go any further. I believe in you.

If you have lived by the principals in SELL·LEARN·REPEAT and tried your hardest to follow the process, and you still aren't getting the results you want, or you are drinking the SELL·LEARN·REPEAT, but don't think your organization can make the leap without outside help, then by all means, feel free to reach out to my assistant's assistant.

And if I have time, and your cause is just, and organic sales growth is critical to the survival and success of your enterprise, and your most senior leadership has bought in, and you didn't blow all your money on focus groups, market studies or Tony Robbins, then I may consider helping you.

But, it will be with a heavy heart and an even heavier wallet.

And if I show up, be forewarned, shits going to get real in a hurry.

Here is another bonus blank page for notes, or if you are using an e-reader, then perhaps some quiet reflection.

TATER THOUGHTS

"What you have to do and the way you have to do it is incredibly simple. Whether you are willing to do it is another matter."

Peter Drucker

www.ingramcontent.com/pod-product-compliance
Lightning Source LLC
Chambersburg PA
CBHW071455220526
45472CB00003B/804